I0529379

JONAH'S MAP OF THE WHALE
AND OTHER POEMS

JONAH'S MAP
OF THE WHALE
AND OTHER POEMS

ANTHONY DOYLE

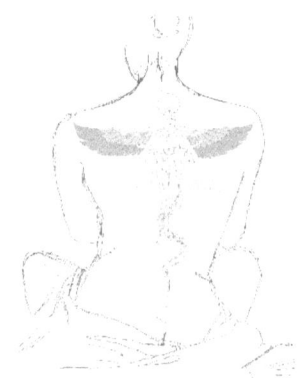

JONAH'S MAP OF THE WHALE
AND OTHER POEMS

Copyright ©20205 by Anthony Doyle. All rights reserved.
Published by Old Scratch Press, an imprint of Current Words Publishing,
LLC. Dianne Pearce, publisher.

This is a work of fiction. Any similarities between actual persons, places, or
events is entirely coincidental.

ISBN: 978-1-957224-54-1 (paperback)
ISBN: 978-1-957224-55-8 (eBook)

LCCN: 2025934408

oldscratchpress.com
currentwords.com

Dedication

To Lara and Branca

To Nico

To the Whale

Also by Anthony Doyle

Hibernaculum (Out of This World Press)

O Lago Secou (Companhia das Letrinhas)

O Livro das Sereias Surpreendentes (Grua)

Contents

JONAH'S MAP OF THE WHALE
AND OTHER POEMS

ONE
Flounder

O'Keano's

O'Keano's fish 'n' chips,
a neon lighthouse, beacon for drunken fish.
Outside, the basking sharks buzz the monument,
raking gusts of rain, somnambulant as nightshade,
rocking parked cars with their REM tails.

And, with a jangling bell, time stops still:
       Molly stumbles on the step
       coming through the door.
       Brent oil for eyeshade,
       a scar on her lower jaw,
       seaweed in the cups
       of her push up bra.
       She scuttles to the counter,
       with barnacles for knees,
       and orders up a fillet,
       when you're ready, pretty please.

       Now, Flounder watches
        as she wades on by,
       converting her to memory
       with his migrant eye.
       Her white-water perfume,
       her midwater chic,
       a pool of rosy wonder
       on her abalone cheek
       For sweet Molly shimmers
       like a Caribbean reef,
       luring life from all around,
       drawn from bluetone deep.

Yes, she gives him moonswell every single time.
A rush of plankton to the head, like salty gallows wine.
She is bathypelagic magic summoned from a trench,

15

with fingers like piano keys and eyes that never blench.
       Her aura runs in flickers
       up and down her spine,
       luciferins bursting
       rhythmical as rhyme.

She's too much sea for a tub like him
Too much sand for his shore.
Yes, he's heard it *all* before.
Where Flounder's from
the only place to look is up.
Things of the world are seen
for the light they block.
But Molly gleams like metal,
Molly twinkles like a star,
a mermaid made in heaven,
to be worshipped from afar;
a mermaid from the heavens,
an angel from below,
her roe rich as stardust
in drifts of neon glow.
And Flounder cannot bear to look
but somehow has to stare.
One day perhaps she'll see him
solidify in air.

Messerschmitt Palace

Along the pier base,
between the dillisk
and the carageen,
among the snagged hooks
and lost tackle,
that is Flounder's home.
He'd prefer a sunken warplane,
say a Messerschmitt, or a spitfire.
Something with history, with *oomph*.
He could live in a wreck like that,
a foundering blunder compressed
      into a mold, shaping
into a reef, breaking
      under the waves, drawing
fish in rings, in roving visitations
      from blue yonder, down
where things can never be red
(Yes, light's a hero in space,
but drowns like a puppy,
much like a Messerschmitt).
But there are no such wrecks here.
No glory stories—many mysteries,
a lot of fantasy, a little shore-porn:
the guilty secrets of a seabed
with the sheets kicked off,
when the wrack drapes in knotty crops,
and the shore—unwaxed, unwashed,
skirts hitched—dreams of gone tides.
You really shouldn't look,
but it's the intertidal zone,
the dregs of sleep and vigil.
Oh, he could squat in a Messerschmitt:
Daimler-Benz long scattered,

canon planted in the bed,
propellers curled like ribbons,
the nose-cone, a septum hole.
The cockpit, void; the camouflage,
borrowed from a white shark,
faded to barnacle. And the fins
—caudal, ventral—snapped,
strewn, a buried archipelago of rivets
and sheet metal. But it wears
      a broken grin, gill to gill.
Yes, he could live in a Messerschmitt,
playing Hamlet to a Lost Soldier's skull.

Dance Night at the Boathouse

On dance nights at the boathouse,
a string of lightbulbs, a whiskey-barrel band.
Perfumes and pheromones wrangle
and jostle like volatiles from
strange African leaves. They mingle,
and some sour in the smoky air.
Others trick with delay, and bloom late,
but most don't wear their skin well.
Seepage from the pores confuses them.
But on dance nights at the boathouse
the voices, the laughter, he listens in,
he laughs at the intonation of jokes
whose words the wind redacts.
The wind that harasses the string
of lightbulbs, strung between masts,
but not the wreathes of stars or the milky moon,
wearing tonight a gala shade of white,
a candid coat, a starchy alb, a naughty pair
of pantyhose. And Flounder wrote:
(no Moleskine, just foolscap)
Moony Molly, Molly Moon,
in my parallel world
you put the boys and the girl to bed
and come and stand beside me by the fire,
your soft hand on my manly shoulder,
you dressed in something satin or silk, and I'll
put down my book, something Greek, and I'll
take off my spectacles, and look into your face.
A cup of tea before bed? you'll say.
A teacup, on a saucer, in a gala shade of white.
One bulb or two? Incandescent,
buoyant in a cup of Irish sea.
And then the wind rounding the pier, it blusters,
blows us both away. Blows you away, and I

the other way, the upside-down I,
and it leaves me here,
like a whelk on a rock.

I can't see you, now, through the crowd,
but you're dancing, I know.
There's a hand on the small of your back,
I know. I can see his eye
on your naked shoulder, and I say
thank you, love, for the tea,
and now I am rather tired.
Shall we turn in? Perhaps
I can brush your hair for you.
Could you, would you
sink with me
into my mattress of sand?
I'll cover us both
in blankets of silt.
Molly, Molly, nose
like a border collie. Don't
let them ever, I'll never
let them, I never did let them,
but they said it anyway.
　　　　They don't now.

Flo_under

Concave convex concave
swimming in Mexican waves
of fin, more like a whale
than a fish, with up and downward flicks
Hovering. Hoovering,
A bottom feeder.
An upward glancer,
An undulating, demersal dancer.
"I am buried a hundred times a day.
Need I say more?"
And he does it to himself.
Instinct elevated to strategy.
He does it to himself.
Sewn into his mattress,
periscopic eyes popping out.

Fanboy Flounder (*Übermenschenaffe*)

"Then history will be divided into two parts: from the gorilla to the destruction of God, and from the destruction of God to…"
"To the gorilla?"
"…to the physical changing of earth and man."

Fyodor Dostoevsky
Demons

Fernando Pessoa said it best:
"Myth is the nothing that is everything."
Hephaestus is the no-one who makes everything.
His product is always in high demand.
His person, not so; his presence, not so.
It's the soul in the tech they want.
Not the lame god with the dribbling cock.
The worst mothers will always expect the best,
as hard to please as they are to redeem.
They truck no weakness, forgive no defect.
And Hephaestus has both of those in spades.
But give the artist a cave with an anvil
and he'll pound something out. Things will become.
All the glorious works of Hephisto:
abetting desires with fated outcomes;
grumbling like the god in the volcano;
like Geppetto in the whale. And Flounder,
who is neither fully puppet nor boy,
broods in his lair round the back of the pier,
biro for a hammer, the words clanging
on his foolscap, protesting as they're shaped.
He cools their glow in the sea, with a hiss,
thinking all the while in blooms of iron and slag:
        "Prometheus of Antiquity,
        altermundial pioneer,
        caught in possession of stolen fire;
        nicked with a swag of hacked intel.

Odysseus of Modernity, CEO,
defrauder of Sirens; could lose a trireme
of good men and still call it a win.
Kings and titans acting like gods
will get us only so far, then frustrate.
But a god who behaves like a man
and makes no promises, foists no rules,
that's an idol for the age
of lowered expectations,
   and stormy weather!
Hephaestus brought more than fire,
he brought forge.
Not only light,
but metal, not just warmth
but weapons; stole the rib
of memory
and made imagination,
made them whole
   in Pandora,
with her jar of naughty dreams:
stars poured from a pithos
of black night; the crystals
of awe in the oils of woe."
It's the dialectic of disappointment.
The real Zarathustras sit quietly in corners.
The *Übermenschenaffe* pays his taxes.
He'll have the new world online
before dismantling the old,
and oversee a seamless transition,
no bluster, no pose.
The *Übermenschenaffe* sees through the veils
but still grooms his kind, picking the ticks,
bursting them on his tongue,
swallowing the blood
with thanksgiving.

Drama Queen of Broken Hearts

Drama queen of broken hearts
       weeping, gnashing,
Nothing less than an eye
       for these front teeth!
Rejection: the hurt for which there is no revenge,
       and little relief.

Flounder skulks by the wallstubs of the ruined castle,
Sulks round the gravel-gray back of the pier,
gasping in tidal pools among the rocks,
where teardrop crabs scuttle across hard cheeks.
       He mourns and mopes—for himself, over her:
       Her?
       Never in a blue February moon.

Flounder is a ghost who haunts his own home
       with flesh, and scales,
       not the turned wood of someone's love,
       or the plasmic threads of another's loss,
       just fins, and the three mouths of fish.

There is comfort in beer cans—*tish*!
       in a suck of ire
       a wheezy puff of no, *no*, No!
       in the hacked phlegm
       of chagrin.

Pity is an embarrassed rebuff:
       'I'm flattered, I am, but…'
… the beauty in her sinkhole eyes,
       macerating, entirely pounding,
leaving Flounder flattened
under a thousand atmospheres of mortification,
       flattened

under an incubus of Irish Sea,
      flattened
by a djinn a whole world heavy,
      squatting on his chest
      and poking at his chin.

Now, Flounder's sadness won't be seen in public
      as anything other than sneer,
but here, in the sealit night,
      it fizzes with imagination,
in plays staged in the sketched space
      of fantasy,
penned in the shorthand
      of mind.
And his drunken performance,
      delivered from the stormwall,
thrums with an odd breed of pride.
The kind that dies in a swamped liver
      and a dried brain.

Leg cocked on a bollard,
finger aimed sure
at the doubled moon,
      he vows:

'The shoe will be on the other foot.
Just you wait and see.
But the shoe will be on the other foot'.

      and down below
      in sublittoral dark,
      the thought of Molly,
      always deimatic,
      thrills with shimmer
      and a puff of ink
      and settles in the sand
      unseen.

Flounders

The mullet shoal along the wharf wall,
stirring teal-green water,
             playful, and oblivious.
Flounder watches from the mud floor.
Light shafts wobble in disturbed murk.
Eight minutes through space for this,
to drown, uncertain, in an Irish estuary.
The rays dust the fish with silver,
but merely pro-forma; there's no bravado left.

Flounder wouldn't know either way.
He's only ever had rhythmic undulations
and silt-bed camouflage.

Topside, mid-afternoon,
perched on a guano-soiled bollard,
he flicks a spent fag-end and watches it flow.
It glides inland between the hulls of rowboats,
rotates clockwise off a mooring rope.
Each discarded butt is lost money and time,
neither of which he will get back.
The smoke of it dissipates in the air,
and he sighs a long goodbye.

Flounder the man cannot see the flatfish,
and the fish can see only the shadow of the man.

Something unsayable binds them in overlap,
and something unspeakable prowls round the edges.

All the things we choose to ignore.
A Council of Nicaea of rational bishops,
excising dissonant shades of reality.

Up at the castle ruins
(mere stumps on a bluff),
Flounder gazes seaward across the cliffs.
The shoreface is framed by a remaining arrow loop.
Its black stone, cold to the touch,
slows his time down, packs it into observable units,
Like drops from a leaking tap
tick, tock,
    drip,
        drop
        Flounder the flatfish darts between sand beds,
        the seaweed flattening in his wake.
        A compass jellyfish, like a fancy desk lamp,
        decorates the half-light, where a dogfish sleeps.
        Flounder beds down as an eel writhes by,
                He waits,
                periscope eyes turning,
                tracking the dark, slender sway.

Summer.
Each one has its visual identity, its theme-tune,
its *dramatis personae*... its narrative.
Its expectations drowned in rain pools.
Summer adores youth.

Flounder sits in the gravel and lights another smoke.
He is too old to be that young, but too young to be this old.
What was supposed to go in-between lay beyond his reach.
It wasn't always thus.
He wasn't always flat.
He wasn't born with his right eye on the left side of his face.
Asymmetry like this starts at a certain age.

        The boy was another fish entirely.
        The *boy* swam upright.

In his dreams, Flounder herds sheep.
He cuts their hooves off, and keeps them underground
in boxes, where no wolves prowl.
He sometimes carries them about on his shoulders,
and knits socks with their wool.
Once, he dreamt of a vigorous man
who came and took the lids off all his sheep pens.
The bleating could be heard throughout the night,
at a depth of three hundred feet.

     The flatfish heard it.
     The flatfish, too, saw the man.
     The flatfish had never seen a sheep.

Flounder used to fear God.
He tried to keep clean a soul
that does not stain like trouser knees,
Does not snag like pullovers
Does not wear bullet holes
Like army parkas, does not
fade in the wash, or wear thin
at the elbows. He did his best
to keep it clean, but sins are like burr
on a linen shroud. The soul
is a linen shroud, and the priests,
they see burned Jesuses on every soul
They see blood stains from zounds,
and we all—all our souls—carry pollen
from Jerusalem, and we all—all souls—
have been scorched in medieval fires.

He tried to keep it clean.
He prayed for cleanliness,
He repented, and tried to scrub
and scrub till his hands were raw,
and the skin cracked round the knuckles

and bled.
And now? Here, at the pier-side,
by the lighthouse, by the harbor wall
he has haunted far too long,
There is no God, and there never was
a soul.

There is no soul, and there never was
a God.

    Flounder watches the shadows
    cross the pale glow of the surface.
    He sees in wrap-round panorama,
    a spread of sea-floor.
    Flounder had never seen a sheep,
    or a God, or a soul. Strange
    that they should be kept in boxes,
    their feet clipped, their blood
    drying all around them. Odd
    that they all bleat the same way,
    and so very, very loud.
    Where is the man to lift all the lids?
    Who is that man?
    On dark nights, Flounder sees pretty lights
    deep in the ocean, lights that dance and pulse,
    rhythmically, and flicker in the blackness.
    In the depths, where he will sometimes go,
    such things are not uncommon. In the depths
    life makes all its own light.

Flounder Walks the Shore

Doc soles crunch the greyscale
The armored interstice
of feldgrau dashed with charm pink
and polished clast veined with quartz.
Yet the eye always finds the sea-glass,
the glinting ambers and greens
of a shore lined with rocks,
dulled, like pinniped teeth.

Flounder picks through the strands
Of wash-up and blowback
Of driftwood and anchor rope
Of tackle and torn nets.
He picks through the strands of wrack
Seeking only surprise.
Surprise, and nothing more.

But here the only color is litter:
The shards and the ribbons
of glass and tin, of labelled
happiness distilled in fluid ounces,
The sucked butts of burnt moments
The Dali-melted sheaths,
          full of still-wriggling time.
All of it flung out and shooed back
          unwanted.

There's a song worn down to the bare notes
Down to the shining bone.
No voice, no arrangement,
Just a groan
Like sheets of metal straining at the bolts.

The soundtrack of shore, perhaps,

Of the threshold mind.
Either waking or dozing.
Never wakeful, never quite asleep.

It's the song of advancement and retreat:
The ebb and rise of time,
The tick and tock of sea.
And Flounder knows it well.

Not in content, only form.
The constant beyond flux:
What surprises, changes; but there is always surprise
Beauty changes, but there is always beauty
Morals change, but there is always morality
Certainties change, yet certainty remains.
But happiness, contentment, satisfaction?
These are contents that never match their forms,
Seas that never reach imagined shores.

And Flounder knows this all too well.
Up above, down below, in-between.

His mother once told him:
Flounder, my boy.
Not a single atom you were born with remains.
Not a single atom in you today was there five years ago.
Not one atom of you now came out of me.

Flounder changes, but there is always Flounder.

Flounder's Photographic Memory

Different past times,
like stains on microscope slides,
click into place in the mind:
Cars modernize, colors sharpen,
trees disappear, and pop up elsewhere.
Walls rearrange…
80s, 90s, click, click, millennium.
Names change on the storefronts.
Storefronts change behind the names.
Pac-man banks are swallowed up,
chemists turn to pharmacies, turned
to drugstores.

And he's still here, all Goth hair and eyeliner,
between the dillisk and the carrageen,
still smoking round the back of the pier
in his army parka, with its fake bullet holes.
No, Flounder. No soldier died in your coat.
Not in Normandy, nor Vietnam,
Not in the Falklands, nor the Persian Gulf.

In O'Keano's on a dole-splurge night
80s pop still plays, and glam rock,
but these are relics, and Molly *née*
doesn't live here anymore.
Someone came and took her away.
Other sylphs slip on this step now
          (retiled, reset),
they float in neoprene,
and preen in plastics.

The future never came.
The past just got longer.
Queuing memories stare
through the backs of each other's eyes.

TWO

Blundra

Blundra Gets News-sick

"If God is the code of the universe, he needs a security patch,"
said Blundra, with exasperation and a little spite.
"Too many exploitable vulnerabilities."
She closed her news app with an angry prod and sighed,
shook her head at the sins of her kind, and closed her eyes.

Grand-mama shuffled in the synapses of oblivion,
smiled discreetly through the surface of a pond,
where koi paraded the fins and scales of time.
She spoke, as always, only in ripples:
"Free will is either a misnomer, or supreme irony,
but it is nevertheless a glitch".

"A bitch?"

"A glitch, dear. A rude and preposterous witch".

Blundra's Spread of Investments

The portfolio manager emailed
from across the felt-topped table,
      hexagonal, with four legs,
      three stretchers,
      one diagonal.
The spread lay out before her:
      positions in cups,
      positions in wands and swords,
      positions, especially, in coins.
Dosed aggression,
      well-aimed caution,
            stubborn heels dug in.
"The good investor, Blundra,
      is like the Chimera:
      part lion,
      part snake,
      part goat.
Attend to the future.
      It's all we've got".
"Attend, too, to the past, my dear,"
      said Grand-mama
      from the shade of a painted rock.
"It's all there's ever been."

Blundra felt a sudden urge
      to dance barefoot
      on the plush tabletop.
An anti-clockwise jig
      with skirt-spin.

Blundra Breaks a Fin

Chasing prey along a rocky shore
full of storefronts, and supermarket trolleys,
pop-up stalls, and elderly shoppers
lost between gondolas,
requires lightning reflexes.
A mermaid must spin, bank, lift and duck
with millisecond speed and stealth.
Clip an aisle corner, and it's off
                  into the fan corals.
Bump a trolley, and you're wrapped
                  in kelp.
The slightest lapse can send you into the jaws
                  of a chauvinistic shark.
Yes, mermaiding is not for the fainthearted,
or absentminded, or lily-livered.
Focus is key in 4D environments.
                  Blundra knows her oceans
                  Blundra knows her moves.
Yet danger comes from where one least expects it:
a diving seabird; a bike courier, a juvenile cookie-cutter…
Those can really ruin a good tail.
                  But sometimes it's a simple guard rail
that catches you, snags you in a fin ray, or a sharp spine.
The pain is spasmic, a shrieking ulnar thrum.
Now Blundra's bundled by the frozen shrimp,
rubbing a pelvic fin, cheeks blown out like a pufferfish.

An elderly triton watches with a sympathetic smile,
limps into the longshore, and is carried out of sight.

Blundra Receives Some Folksy Wisdom

Awake and check the mountain
　　　　for signs of mood, elation, grump.
Mien means an awful lot
　　　　with mountains.
They know the day before it breaks.

The riverbank at dawn is a true place,
　　　　the water has seen all future clouds.
They glide there first, before the sky.
　　　　All weather
Derives from the shadows of fish.

And be sure to give the wind a sniff.
　　　　It's either felling or spreading.
A whiff's enough to glean the which,
　　　　though it's best
Not to meddle in the wind's affairs.

If two of the three defer,
　　　　stay inside and mind your hearth.
Attend to inner business,
　　　　obey the day.
It will not bend to your wiles.

But if the mountain smiles,
　　　　the fish show their backs,
　　　　the wind blows easy,
Waste none of time's good time.
And if the mountain scowls,
　　　　the river flows closed,
　　　　the wind changes tone,
Waste none of time's bad time.
And most of all, don't forget to wake.

Blundra Returns from the Desert

Industry, the fallen art,
consumes with zeal, diligently.
Red as Mao, with a Lenin goatee.
Its horns in the Hamptons
Tail swishing in the quays,
slapping at the metal hulls
of groaning ships.

endostre conquered the world,
Trampling the earth
with cerium hooves,
Turning the rocks into focaccia,
stones into scones. Always

turning something into something else.
Samemade, madesame.

And the captains of ūstrī,
sun shining out their asses,
jump off St. Patrick's spire
and don't even stub a toe.

Horns in Manhattan,
Forked tail in Detroit car yards.

'But that's not the worst:
He took me up, once,
onto Lion King's rock
in Silicon Alley
and he says: all of this belongs to me.
As far as the eye can see,
it's all mine,
and I can give it to whomever I please.
Just go down on me.

Go down on your hands and your knees.

Horns in California,
Tail beating like a slow, tired fan
in a Chinese sweatshop.

Double dare, double dare:
If you are so shit shit hot
Send your car into outer space.
Grow a heart from a spot in a dish.
Clone your dog, your mother,
a shoal of mislabelled fish.

Horns in the Cloud,
Tail deep in some African mine.

Blundrices

I.

Blundra fumbled among deep structures,
  her hand in the biscuit tin of old mind.

  She fished out an instinct, ancient as a therapsid,
  which rolled over and played dead, thwarting the kill.

Good thing / bad thing want/not want
  take into your mouth, or clamp shut and wince.

  Taste or not to taste? But she knew this already:
  She could feel the memory of it in her spittle, haunting her palate,
  graffitied on her tongue, a shadow cast.

    So Blundra rolled over,
      played dead,
      thwarted the kill;
    arm recalled from the biscuit tin,
    made for hands with opposable thumbs.

II.

Blundra's old school friend found her on social media,
  liked a post showing fireflies in Blundra's garden at night,
  then left a comment like an invitation.
  Killie, one eye larger, or slightly lower slung, great big woolly hands
    with retractable claws. Sweet heart, honest to a fault.
    Terribly afraid of the dark.

  Blundra helped Killie with math:
    "Don't forget, do what's in parentheses first."
  One day, musing over banana sandwiches,
    Killie remarked:

"It's a life lesson, that…
When you're stuck and don't know what to do,
just look for the parentheses.
There's always parentheses,
and that's where you start."

(Blundra has long seen something there are no words to say.
It's been there for years; not silent,
but outside of silence and sound,
in brackets of nowhere, waiting.)

III.

Blundra sniffs books.
She does.
She opens them with glee,
Hoovers in their scent:
      Ah!
      windrush and oak bark, with a touch of bile and squalene,
      a note of whetstone, and of scorched battlement,
      smoked in campfire, and set, if I'm not wrong, in pine sap.

She runs her finger along the spines like the bones of ancient animals,
      some disgorged from faultlines, others from the shallowest graves.
Her shelves are a cabinet of human curiosities,
      tiny deformities preserved in the formaldehyde of tale.

IV.

Blundra's mother is an orca, tail-batting seal pups for fun,
lacrossing them high into the air.

Blundra's mother is the gazelle that gave one lick,
then left her foal to the leopard's maw.

But Blundra learned to swing from those fangs
and to make the big cat laugh.

She mastered the triple half-twist pike,
and can smile through seal-pup eyes.

Blundra's mother is a memory;
a will-o'-the-wisp at the roadside.

V.

Blundra's imaginary friend
      had many enemies.
She spoke too much truth
      to be free;
too much reality
      to dwell in the real world.

Blundra's imaginary friend,
      who took tea in the attic
      and played chess out on the porch,
knew too many secrets
      to roam in the open.
She knew all mother's thoughts
      and father's feelings.
She knew the lovers in one neighbor's bed,
      and the graves in another's yard.

They got to her, in the end,
Blundra's imaginary pal...
Compromised by a therapist,
she L-pilled in a rowing boat on Lake Anza,
and sank into the water, real as a stone.

Blundra on a Winter Wednesday (Wakersgrave)

Blundra stares into a wintry morning.
Latte in-hand, super-hot, heat
hammering through the cup-holder.

She walks into the risen wind,
a phoenix from the bay,
and on through background streets,
her footfall always at optimal arcs.
She leans into clipping points
on corners, and accelerates
into busy, store-lined straits,
her mind a balloon tethered to the skull,
as she makes her way to work.
On the bridge, a half-heeded thought
dies on its run from a private Marathon:
there's something in the air we have forgotten how to see.
It pounds on the innards of the brain
like a stranger's fist on the window.

Confident she strides
between the cliffs of graphene steel
and reflective glass, as the mellow sun
shimmers on the frosted panes,
the cold water, the hot car-hoods.

There it is again, the satisfied sigh of history:
         Echo, almost only white gleaming bones.
         Narcissus, just handprints in the lakeshore mud.

Blundra rides the elevator, bracing for the spill-out,
for the onrush, for the phonespeak and power suits.
For the busied field of vision.

She slinks from the lift-mouth, glides across the raised floor
(where the veins thrum with electric blood),
slumps into her swivel chair for another day of code.

Blundra: absorbed in her work,
expressed in her absorption,
rewarded by its expression,
a conduit for the sounds that no-one makes:
The basophils of increment, leucocytes of firewall.
Not quite Voynichese, but a Hebrew of modernity.

And Blundra is sewn into the leg of modernity.
She hatches daily from the head of world, then brushes her teeth.
But she does not host the tongue-replacing louse of her time.

[lunch break: biodegradable tray with 10 slices of farmed shrimp and mango roll, with
hot sencha tea]

The mind does not wander.
It gets tugged around by unseen guides

      here

                  there

        the

          eye

             a   planchette.

        The   mind,

             it   never

wanders.

      It's always following something

The treebirds are singing
    in the park.
The parkbirds are singing
    in the trees.
A wren trillbeeps and scolds,
    loudball, so light,
barely even there at all,
    this puff of wren.
And Blundra recalls an old legend
about a dragon in its den.
A dark tale etched in memory
and steeped in lore.
The story of a barren mineland
told by Grand-mama.
She called it Wakersgrave,
for there the people rose each day
to mourn another stolen child,
snatched from bed linen, from cot swaddle,
snapped from a sleeping mother's arms
with drooling stealth, with throat-rattle,
and tyrannosaurus grin.
Yes, for there a scaly demon cloaked in night
exacted tax in kin.
This Wakersgrave was a town on a rim,
built on the lip of a coil-pit mine
concentrically bored into the ground.
Their drilled pursuit
    of recoverable carats
had gored through the rock's reserves
    —a diamond paradise—
disturbing the dragon's priceless sleep.
A hundred years it prowled since,
stealing gems for stolen gems,
taking eyes for teeth.

Feathered this in leafless that
Scrawls upon the sky.
A craquelure of twittery,
and little Blundra, seven,
"Don't open them till I tell you".
Eight O'Clock Hallowe'en night.
Face paint and fake blood.
Nuts and apples bobbing
in a basin. Nine friends
in a coven of giggle
(A philter for Phillip;
some Henbane for Harriet).
Salt lakes and dustblow
across the surface of a sink hole.
Flamingo flock, guano.
The volcano ejaculates
on Mamma Mountain
and life gestates underground.

Blood	*Rain*	*Sperm*
Red	*Black*	*White*
Lights	*Wind*	*Shapes*

The sunhand ticks across the horizon:
Mountain, volcano, mountain, volcano, mountain
Seasons stretch and shorten like shadows
Blood

        Black

                Shapes

| *Diamonds* | *Diamonds* | *Diamonds* |

fixed in monocular stare.
Purity is valued in all but people.
Expect no flawless gems.
Minedirt on megatruckbacks, 400-ton hauls.
How many recoverable carats?
How many recoverable souls?

"Oh angels on high
      please hear our prayer.
Vanquish the monster
      in its dankest lair.
For we are good
      and God is fair."

Heavenwards rose their souls' despair
and angels harked their doleful plea.
None could ignore without a care
such piteous entreaty.
A malakh donned cuirass and helm,
and plunged through starlight tide and whelm.
descending to earth, realm after realm,
      to set the townsfolk free.

He crashed to land not far from where
the mine pit curled below the ground,
and raised his sword into the air
as rain burned all around.
"I heard your call and feel your pain,
see your needs and know your bane
and shall not rest till it is slain",
then vanished underground.

The miners felt the wide plain shake,
their wives, their earthware fall.
The land atremble, cramped in quake,
lay braced in a murky pall.
Far below where shadows bloom,
torchlight-born in death's dark womb,
the duel continued, draped in gloom,
      a wild and murderous sprawl.
At last they burst into the skies,
angel and beast, locked in war.

Jewels for the plush-trays of Paradise?
Do unto others as you would (ye, the powerful),
Or as they have done unto you (ye, who strive),
Or as you would have them do unto you (ye, that fear
and tremble).
Do the dead become angels, Grand-mama?
'Ach! Angels know nothing of death.'
Young Blundra prays with cathedral hands,
Spires of fingers, thumb tympanum, arched
Like whale ribs.
'Deliver us, Lord. Spit us from the gullet,
For we spy through the blow-hole.
Deliver us from evil, for we so wish to do it'.
The soul is self-imagining in life
and self-remembering in death.
How many diamond moments in a life?
How many recoverable carats?
One per two tons of rock removed, if that…
Ah, the gemlike scarcity of moments
worthy of such eternity.
'Ten, be back by ten. You're only eleven, remember?'
But at 12 o' clock, Blundra was still snogging
a vampire round the back of the YC.
Grounded for 14 days, until Friday 13th.
But it was worth it, for a carat.
You've only go fifteen seconds
to make a first impression, see.
So she chased him round the dance floor
with a stake.

There is the violence of angels
and the violence of devils.
They both hurt the same, and no worse
than the violence of schmucks'.
Evil is in the eye of the beholder,
Because we know it when we see it, whether

The people cried and hid their eyes,
astounded by the roar.
Those beating wings gathered a cloud,
obscuring all in a bitter shroud,
as on they battled, high and proud,
      spattered now in gore.

Till the dragon was no more.
Smitten through its core.

The town erupted with such cheer,
scarcely believing the deed was done.
The dragon skewered with a spear,
the angel's battle won.
Libations frothed through the night,
The minefolk drunk on sweet delight,
and none retired till day's first light
      was spilled by the rising sun.

But before dawn, as night withdrew,
the grey plains glistened, moist with dew
as all around the morning's breath
dispelled the coldest stench of death.
And no man saw what happened then:
The dragon stirred to life again.
No more a beast, but a simple wren,
      and into town it flew,

Where lambs were being bled and burned
sending skyward grateful plumes.
The grace received was thrice returned
in sacrificial fumes.
The angel readied his ascent,
borne upon this message sent,
and the nimble wren, on vengeance bent,
      in his feathers fast inhumed.

JONAH'S MAP OF THE WHALE

angel   *demon*   *schmuck*
light   *wind*   *shape*
They each have their weapons,
and each has their words,
which never miss,
and cannot be dodged.

Lightning cuts the cloud's belly.
The rain wets the dry land.

No males in Blundra's family photos.
The males are dead or otherwise gone.
Family is a feminine noun, a dialectic.
Blundra tiptoes round the quicksand,
the dark matter of mother.
Blundra clings to the warm light,
to the safe glow of Grand-mama,
morphing into octahedron, compressed
like a plucked flower, under 200kms of pages,
melted and re-crystallized as ghost.
One and a half billion years of time
worn upon her ring finger most of a lifetime long.
One carat — two tons of moved earth—
in an 18k handcrafted platinum band,
a triumph of artistry, yet all in vain,
as he was taken by a diamond in the colon,
A rough diamond that cleaved and cleaved.
Grand-père, Michel, Michel, archange…
Smitten through his core.
Alchemy of sacrifice:
Earthly flesh and blood <to>
Heavenly word and light,
translated by the serpents of smoke
in vertical communications.
We feed our gods like geriatrics,
Pleadingly, in priestly aprons:

The malakh climbed on heaven's stair
and off across the upper seas,
past wild orbs and the sun's bright flare,
obtaining Rakia with ease.
And on he flew through gates thrown wide,
Along the gilded mountainside,
and crossed the city at a glide
      upon a peaceful breeze.

The wren perused the land below
and spied an ancient tree aside,
an oak with leaves of mellow glow
and veins of fire inside.
Detaching from its angel host
it fluttered, subtle as a chime,
and settled in that bough, topmost,
to bide the auspicious time.

Alighting on a slender spray
the wren inhaled and puffed its chest,
then burst into song so shrill and gay
it stirred the citadel from rest.
A crowd was drawn unto that grove
by wren bewitched, and on it throve,
in trill and chirrup, magic it wove
      within its gentle breast.

The warring angel, hated foe,
his armor stained with dragon's blood,
knelt by the tree, and bowing low,
Implored:
"Oh, mirthful bird, if you would:
How can it be that paradise—
perfection pure—can still devise
such preternatural surprise?"

'Just a little more, Grand-mama,
then we're good till the solstice".
Grand-mama was silent; blue eyes staring,
Lips pursing, gently moving.
It hurt to eat, so she drooled.
'Blundra, when will you grow your hair out?
You were so very pretty with long hair.
You look like Jean d'Arc all cropped.'
Grand-mama, if the universe is expanding,
what is it expanding into? A Nothing that depletes?
A Something else that shrinks?
I fear it can't end well.
'Always the pessimist, my girl'.
No, a realist. 'Yes, like I said,
Always such a pessimist.'
I'm a realist, Grand-mama!
'Yes, a nihilist, with short hair'.
Grow your innocence long and flowing
Your locks of grace thick and glowing,
Strands of kindness, in bouncing rays.
Down the blindingly white tunnel,
wrensong rebounding, heart light
as a feather, flying on wren wings.
Grand-mama, grand-mama, her heart
light as a feather
            within her gentle breast.

Perfection cannot change. To do so, and still be perfect
would require plural possible perfections.
A contradiction.
The Perfect, as immutable, must therefore be constant,
and nothing in nature is constant,
so nothing in nature is perfect.
If Heaven is perfect, then Heaven is unchanging,
and so closed to all additions.

and silence filled the wood.

The wren approached and tapped its beak
upon the fiery, ancient bark;
combusted with a baleful shriek
and spread its wings across the park.
Transformed anew as dragon wild
it sought the angel it reviled,
and some would swear it even smiled,
      as the square entire went dark.

It crept upon him, slow and sure,
its fires rekindled, flushing red;
its mind awash with thoughts impure,
all trace of churring wren now shed.

The angel drew still dripping sword.
The dragon bared its fangs and roared,
then, stepping forth, seized its reward,
      and struck the angel dead.

      Jaws ripping off his head.
      Lips grinning while it bled.

The body's light dispersed in rays,
The armor filled with searing haze.
The angels stared in disbelief,
      overcome with grief.
The dragon took to screeching flight
erasing trees with fiery blight,
it wasted swathes with such delight,
      torching leaf upon leaf.

Descending swift to Wakersgrave
The dragon took that coiling stair

Anything outside of Heaven must therefore not pertain
to perfection, and so be excluded forever therefrom.
An accessible Heaven cannot be perfect
Or cannot be Heaven.
Blundra dreams of imperfect heavens.
Changing heavens, growing heavens,
Frothing with bubbles of memory and dream,
An archaeology of 'I's,
meshed like fullerenes.

Diamond and deep peridotite.
Diamonds and deep-ocean basalt.
Each carat just one-fifth of a gram.
How light, then, is a bird's heart?

In the Land of the Blind, the one-eyed man is king,
But he is also toothless.
Ah, the joys of civilization!
Malleable reality, unwavering will.

Do you remember, Grand-mama,
Our Glossary of Windological Terms?

Hush — the world should sleep now.
Ooooh — surprise; fear
Shoo — Out of the way please!
Swish — do something, I'm bored.
Whoooo—mild interest, or, "Strange things afoot".
Hoof— negativities in general
But mostly the wind just says "Shush".
It rushes back from the ocean, and says:
Shush   Shush   Shush
Coming off the bay, all it says to us is Shush.
When it meets me on the corners,
it will brush against my lips and say **Shush**

returning to its vacant cave
to claim again its ancient lair.
But heaven's choirs, with doubt assailed,
many disturbing truths unveiled,
and grasped the puzzle this entailed,
   now hanging in the air.

  Suspicions everywhere.

Did God all-seeing mark this foe,
and let the demon through the gates?
It's that, or else He did not know
that a fiend in heaven waits.
Discussions roused, and voices raised,
as angels high and low dismayed—
bewildered, undercut, betrayed—
   in vigorous debates.

Our question must be put,
   our fears allayed'.
An answer must be sought!'
   the angels brayed.

Down conjured halls these angels tread
through spaces built by time congealed.
For hours on-end, with mounting dread,
they roamed the master's rooms unsealed,
till a presence made them reel,
   cower down and kneel:
"Forgive us, Lord, for we must ask
how did it come to be
that in our world of heaven
a fiend could pass so free?"

As silence woke around their sound.

All the wind ever says these days is…
…and it's back to the sounds that no-one makes.
Back to the code, and the polished logics
of algorithm and graph.
Back to the sounds the wind never makes.

Shush, shush, shush.

Omniscience excludes error
Omnipotence excludes failure
Omnipresence excludes otherness.
Yet we're told it's all the Devil's fault!?
There was no Fall. That angel was pushed!
          Shush, shush, shush
Do something in life that will want to remember itself
when you're gone.

Like evil you will know it when you see it.
Like beauty it will dispense with words.
Rare as precious stones,
such moments make the wind sigh,
make it whisper.

We know very little of anything
but something of nothing.
Is that what makes us human, Grand-mama?
'Yes, my dear. I suspect it is.'
Will I ever see you again, Grand-mama?
'Anytime you wish'.
I'm afraid the wind will lose its voice without you.
Or my ears will close to its voice without you near.
I'm afraid I'll lose my words
to the tongue-replacing louse of maturity.

'Always the pessimist, my short-haired girl'.

The angels fast withdrew.

Until a voice broke like the dawn:

"I am the morning dew."

'Always the nihilist'.

But I will *see you again, Grand-mama,*

robed in the morning dew.

Blundra's Anatomy

I have a black-walled womb
With gneiss folds and mud floes.
It's all bark too, with trickles of sap
and latex, incubated circles,
and encircled squares, triangles rhombused
in still reflections.
Often, it loses labyrinths
down white rabbit-holes. Yes
I have a black-walled womb
that fosters growth and provides product.
Things run screaming from its gates;
Tumble from its mouth, half drowned.
I lick them clean, like foals.

I have a gaseous heart.
It draws me around itself, holds me about it
in constellate organs, and ribbons of vessel,
in spools of nerve. Such is its gravity,
it throws me around it in expansions of skin,
all flare and mass, as it speaks bright,
and darkens. Speaks bright, and darkens.
Speaks bright, as I spin on my axis,
up-and-down, left-and-right.

I have a teetering brain,
a stacked favela of wind-etched whistles.
Proof that all sound is the marriage
of shape and shapelessness.
What do they see, those windows?
They see me, beheld in existence,
the condensate of eyes.
I try to remember that memory imagined
what fantasy would have me forget.

But I am a black-walled womb.
Warmed by a red-ball heart,
primal swamplife caked in brain.

And my bones are of fossilized trees.

THREE

Jonah's Map of the Whale

The Misadventures of the Finless Vertebrate Alex Iden Gray

Jonah (Nebi Yunus) was sent to the Assyrian city of Nineveh

(Mosul, Iraq) to warn the people to mend their ways or face destruction. He was ridiculed and ignored. Weary and saddened by his failure, he left Nineveh and boarded a ship to Tarshish (Gibraltar). On the way across the Mediterranean, God sent a terrible storm onto the ocean, and the pagan crew feared someone aboard had angered the gods, and that only a sacrifice would appease them. So they drew lots to determine who should be thrown overboard. Three times Jonah drew the short straw, so he was flung into the waves, where a great fish (*dag Gadol*) rose up to snatch him. Swallowed by this fish or whale, Jonah was taken to the depths of the sea, where he was wrapped in darkness and seized by despair. After three days in the whale's belly, Jonah cried out for deliverance or death and was spat back onto the shore. With his skin corroded by stomach acids, the sun stung like venom on his body, yet Jonah returned to Nineveh and waited on the sand outside the city. God ordered a gourd to grow around him and provide shelter and relief, but soon sent a worm to kill the gourd and take back the gift—warning against further complacency. Having seen the fierce storm, and witnessing now the prophet's return in such a transformed state, the people of the great city repented and renounced their old ways.

Sharkbitten

April 23, 2018

Sharkbitten,
turned wet and salty,
shorelined, sandbarred,
he said something
        no-one understood;
something about eastrogen
and westrogen
        about balance,
and environmental services.
He was pump-lung and blue-lipped,
hooked to a drip of paranormalol,
and wrapped in shock blankets.
He could still feel the crunch.

Still, it could've been worse,
he could have been like Paul,
who cracked his skull falling from a horse
one sunny day:
        stretched on the operating table,
        drugged into scenes of pre-frontal nudity,
        they interfered with his damaged Godslobe
        and he was blind thereafter.

Shark attack is a grisly affair:
Estuary, brackish water, chest-high,
a warm, rich swell
silted from days of rain,
a soft breeze
        (just a quick pre-dinner dip,
        habit is no assurance.)
Crawl-stroke, neoprene,
a broken storm limps toward Cuba,

a white line of foam
on the wavebreaker.
He was at home in the sea,
this bipedal, finless vertebrate.
Still, it could have been much worse.
No shame in sharkbite.
But the crunch, oh
the wallop,
and drag.
The chomp.
The popping joint
and elastic snap;
the roll of an eightball eye.
Sandpaper pitbull, all bodywork and cage,
thrashing at the trough in muscular rage.

He floats in the crimson,
catches a lucky wave.

Redshift and sirens in Florida dusk;
angels fold their wings and fall to work
dismantling the set, perched like noble vultures
on Santa Rosa ribs, tearing up the beach
like pasteboard, dropping the housefronts
like stage props, turning off the fans
under plastic waves, and squeezing the air
out of the clouds.
Faceless paramedics work the tourniquet,
Eyeless paramediums fumble for a turnkey.
Mouthless paratroubadors sing the keystone,
and he watches the sky, burnt round the edges,
peel from the vast unknown at one corner,
a sun bubble extrudes and pops like gum,
a rip in the third heaven,
and his body of light,
still tethered by a cord,

roams the white shore,
thumbing the dog-eared waves
as a musty yawn, long and old,
blows from the lighthouse,
and whistles through the sproket holes
of night.

When the new sun rises
it will flake the clouds like paint
and burn all the pages of the sea.
But, for now, the flickering moon,
overexposed, rolls back to mamma
in reverse caesarean. Recombinant sands
crawl into empty letters, and scuttle
across the rocks of hardback shores.
All the weary tales turn to pictures,
moaning as they spill their time
and fall slack.

They came from the east...

Alex is leaving us, Alex is almost gone:
Pearly Gates open for receivership,
angels with six-sigma wings, bailiffs with seven broken seals.
Shock is a frightful thing; those weeds about the head,
the soul fainting.
The bell rings, and is heard by all the creatures of the sea,
as the zeros fall from the board,
scatter across the pit like fruit,
and find the cold pockets of dark pools.

White hallways, asepsis,
 swinging doors…

Through the eye of a needle, a transparent gate of horn,
Morpheus' rivers swell the bloodstream.

Three Visitors

April 24, 2018

Laetoli mud on primitive feet
volcanic ash on tangled hair,
Australopithecus afarensis
gags malodorous, chemical air.

He strokes a stump of severed leg
and stares into a beardless face,
turned taut and pale in bleary light
that gives no measurement of place.

Behind him trails the Iceman Ötzi,
leatherbound like an ancient book,
disgorged from millenary ice
from the folds of an Alpine ruck.

He draws erect his murdered frame
and shuffles in his goatskin coat,
regards awhile the bandaged stump
with gaze familiar and remote.

With the wanderer and southern ape
another waits beside that bed,
a younger man in a desert cape,
a crown of scars around his head.

The three stand at the sleeper's side
and pass along a quart of rum
as Jonah dreams in seaweed lash,
a fainted soul, half-drowned, grown numb.

Three nights he'll wade encaged by ribs
as shallow waters lap his shins.
Three nights and days he'll dream the fish,
defibrillant, in mocking fins.

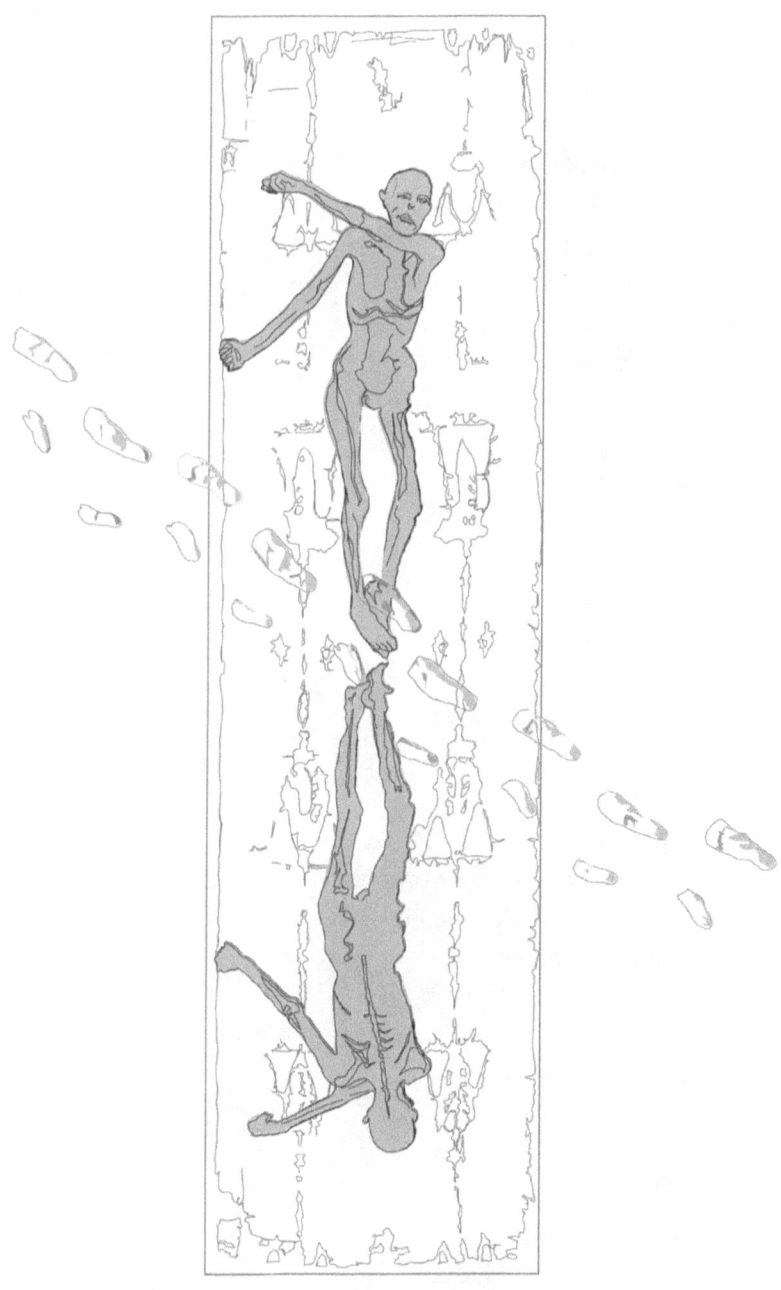

Underwater Magi

December 2016

Bringing to the surface
what would rather dive
       and run deep,
fishing is the oldest art.
The barbed pole, the harpoon,
gillnets, setnets,
geometry and bark twine.
Hooks of snailshell, of carved bone,
of juniper, of bronze.
Hooks, with eyes to see
and points to make.

Before there were crosses to bear
the load of a man was his coracle,
a shell to float in.
The hearth-fire was the first book,
because the best wisdom is eaten.
We dine on our sages:
the bull, the lamb, the fish.

There was once a fishman, Oannes,
emissary of Ea, who,
as the dawn crept above the Zagros Mountains,
would walk from the waters of the Persian Gulf
and speak the culture of men
into their dull, hard heads,
so that those who lived on earth
might dwell in world.
A tale of two prepositions,
earth and world...

Alex is quite the fisherman too.
The terror of trout, bane of bluefish

scourge of the shoreline.
When he emerges from the 30A surf
it's always with a grin and a fish dinner.

Fishing is a craft pursued in craft,
in caskets for the not-yet-dead.
The Inuit used bone or driftwood,
lashing the frames with sinew
wrapped in caribou and sealed with fat.
Today, it's polyethylene, with seatbacks,
and pedals, and cup-holders, kayaks
for plastic Tequesta.

Alex the angler, the pocket jangler, trader and trender, market wrangler.
Alex of triple-A health and wealth, grizzled and chiseled and carefully
svelte. Oannes the fish man, Jonah the whale man, Alex the mereman,
milfman, talisman. Alex the man's man, rich man, purrman. Alex the
überman thinking out-loud. Alex in swaddle, pinstripe, shroud. True to
his code, his creed, his profession, proudly he shares his checklist
confession. But it's not bragging if you look contrite.

Out on the sound, with the blue brushed grey
by gust and cloud, his sleigh bag carries no gifts
this Christmas day, only a speckled trout.
The cold has run the fish deep, or south.
It's rough now, with no patience.
Like the nation, no patience.

A cut mackerel dangles
in a trail of oils and blood.
The bouquet of wound
draws her in:
a black-tip shark,
just shy of forty pounds,
cloaca still unprobed.
She fights and runs,

leaps and tires,
screaming down the reel:

No child in your manger
No child
No son to take your trade
No son
No daughter to give away
No altar
No heir to your throne,
No home,
just a house.
Not Mar-a-Lago,
but a house.

The good life,
Ah, the best life:
all beings, and havings, and doings.

But no child to teach how to fish.
The world is full enough already.
It's a very, very, very full world
Very full.
"Merry Christmas and a very, very, very…"
Too full
"very Happy New Year to everyone"
Then off to prayers at Bethesda-by-the sea:
      In the name of the How
      The Who
      and the Why Bother.
           Amen
Not a throne, but a house.
A winter white house, won by siege.
"And a very, very, very…"
full world, full of
Ghosts of Christmases Past

demanding hush money.

Still she dives,
and fights,
still
she fights
and breaches
twisting in the air.

But none of us can run forever
We all gnaw at the braided line of time,
we all feel the drag of the unyielding reel.

Yet not even Hemingway
would haul an angry shark into a kayak,
so Alex cuts the line.
Off you go now.
There you go....

and the merciful captor
with his quill of debarbed hooks
reclines and sighs,
gazing up at Cetus in the Water,
with her swarm of galactic krill,
her bloom of milky plankton.

Lowslung in the northern sky
where the surface lolls
in a spray of stars, the whale's tail
flicks the night.

The Whale's Belly, 00h 26m 22.2486s– 03h 23m 47.1487s

The Universe Conspires

October 2011

25th day of Dhu al-Qa'dah,

Blue gulf, Santa Rosa, Emerald Coast

Caught between a beachfront and a coastal lake,
one man's dream foreclosed, another's bargain.
Palladian pomp, Carrera marble.
Wide open stairwell, Turkish chandelier.
70 feet of shoreline out the rear,
where white drifts compile on drystick fences.
Poolside, a colonnade, deck chairs, sunshade.
The lawyers stripped his life like a stolen car.
She got their friends, the dog, the brownstone;
He, a mancave with an ocean view:
pool-felt green, reef-tank blue,
  memorabilia in acrylic cases,
  old whiskeys from historic casks,
And on a wall full of screens, all ticker reel
and news feeds, live scenes
from half a world away in smoldering Sirte:

  A crusty copper yellow day
  Oily plumes of smoke uncoil
  Jubilant rebels crowd and shriek
  As nerves and tempers boil.
  The monster caught, found the wretch,
  All Bedouin and royal.

  Bloodied, bitchslapped, showered with grit
  Narrow eyes dulled and glazed.
  The Guide is frogmarched toward a truck
  His tyrant's pomp erased.

No palaces, no comely tent,
All former glories razed.

A freezer room, the corpse displayed
On desert mattress lain,
A shank of beast to slice and share
In pixelated pain,
A third-eye zoom on cold blue wounds,
Recording every stain.

Three days dead, unwashed, unburied,
No kafan, no public prayer.
The crowds queue to see for themselves
To certify and stare,
Be sure that underneath the skin
The soul's no longer there.

And another one gone.
One more domino falls
Because everything ends in dust,
        except dust, which never ends.
Entropy is qualitative gravity.
What structures-up must come down:
Regimes, religions, triple-A credit ratings.
All order succumbs to the chaos it defies,
being only fueled movement before rest.
Ah, success!
There are always those who feed first,
and feed best.
There are no Marxist jungles, no holy savannas,
No socialist seas.
Not even the womb is egalitarian,
        ask the shark pup, the runt cub.
Alex has a lot of order in the bank.
So much order invested,
Some high-risk, some low.

He has remained big enough to fly
but small enough to hide
beneath the eagle's wing,
All the better to escape
when they cleave it straight off.

What's the frequency Alex?
Send it out and it bounds right back
—"you're not a winner because you won,
you won because you're a winner"—
The Law of Attraction:
visualize and you shall receive.
The Universe will conspire
—all hundred billion gigaelectronvolts—
to pull the rabbit from a starry hat.
Dark thoughts breed dark matter,
Positive thoughts, white pearly light.
If you've got it, you earned it
and the universe knows it,
even Hubble can see it,
because it's physics.
The unreasonable munificence of math.
Alex looked into the face of Polly's lawyers
        and lived.
        Lived and prospered.
He's got the power.
He's got the whole world in his hands.
And there's a message that I'm sending out
Like a photograph of the soul.
See you just can't beat persistence
Throw this Jonah overboard.
I ain't kiddin' you at all.
        Yes, it's true.
        He shits you not.
It's the counterclockwise tick
        of churning storms.

A bung in the carbon sink.
Entropy Exports & Cold Storage Inc.
We deliver, free of charge.

Wall Street

September 2008

West-facing windows
       gaze on east-facing windows
       reflecting west-facing windows
licked with gold
       tongues, from stone mouths,
filled with the smoke of alchemy,
       curling into birds,
dark and nightly, wintry,
       flecked with September's
       summer embers,
Forgetful of June flight
          from a nest in May,
back when spring was still spring.
But now autumn yawns in slivers of pink,
blowing shadows stretched and long.
Amongst them, the American International
lolls like a tongue across molar roofs,
slinking toward the waterfront.
A great gothic mountaintop,
its needle sliding through the grooves of cloud,
spilling scratchy music across the orb.
Above the tower's doors radiant pyramids shine,
emblems of the opulence of decay.

At the Stock Exchange,
a house with six columns and seven doors,
where integrity despairs at the works of man,
Alex Iden Gray
buries his face in his hands.

Closed at 4.76 a share.
Hoof-prints of blood on the trading room floor.
The Bull, wet nostrils weeping,

passes briefly one moment on the shore
of another Delphi,
Shakes heavy head at the stalled index
and seething, sweeps the bars in search
of Persephone
      She is fragrant
      she is always sweet
      and needing
Outside, Demeter is bright and calm
      this evening
Her smile bathes all in late summer light
Her breath runs fresh among the tree-boughs

      Lower Manhattan
      A mirror of reflected high-rise light
      A citadel

On Maiden Lane, past Pearl and Gold,
two blocks from where that tower stands,
she sips a cocktail through a straw,
as Alex strokes her velvet hands.
He brushes back her perfect fringe
and fidgets with a briolette
hung chime-like from a pearly lobe,
exacting giggles of regret.
Each chuckle rolls in undertow,
arousing swirls of ocean silt,
which Alex bats with shell-like lids,
as weak defenses start to wilt.
His voice, a slow uncrumpling page,
relaxes with each smoothened phrase:

Come with me, come with me
Down
Come with me into the earth
Come down

Come down with me
into the dark,
and later,
her waters warmed enough for a storm,
as she sucks all the air out of the room,
he waits for the moment to dump his stock,
his participation ending in sequential dots.

A clown fish in an anemone,
He wakes with tailrot
and ick.

Rolls across the stones,
scratches up against a ship.

darts to the surface,
to piss and spit.

six o three am

Dawn light on Brooklyn Bridge
a taxi slips through a brick arch.
His Blackberry chimes:
        "You didn't come home last night…"
His Caneberry chimes:
        "Hammered in Asia…expect below 2.0"
His dewberry chimes:
        "20bn not enough…need Fed"
His Rubus fruticosus chimes, Polly Glottenberg:
        "My divorce lawyer…save the number…"
He thumbs the ripening drupelets in his palm,
squashing out the letters,
staining his fingers with their juice:
        "Don't worry…too big to fail… too interconnected".

Crushed ticks ooze good tock

Those Assyrian Bulls

June 2003

Quadruple witching hour.
A spread of futures and options
in upturned cards and palms,
expiring before our eyes.
Down point-eight-six this second Friday of June.
The witches, done squealing in the empty pit,
straighten their skirts and mount their brooms.

A storm hunkers above the isle,
wind rushes through the busy streets.
Lightning flares behind the cloud,
as thunder tumbles on electric stairs.

In a cab, heading uptown,
Coconuts drop from his Palm Treo:
"Jam on FDR, wait by the Iamassu".

The Metropolitan, second floor, east face:
Assyrian grandeur.
The winged bull and lion of Nimrud,
alabaster guards that flank an arch
stare cold-eyed down a hall of slab reliefs.
He sees her hover by the yellow room beyond,
her silhouette dwarfed by the sculpted beasts.
		Like Ishtar, she kicks at the doors of heaven.
		Like Venus, she is out of bounds until Sunday.
She runs a finger along the bull's cleft hoof
and checks for dust.

Polly, valent and aesthetic,
owner of an unconscious pout,
wonders what is keeping him.

And there he is, as if conjured.
The rain, roadworks, Irish driver,
you know…So you found them then,
the great Assyrian bulls…
No, they found me on the stairs,
asked me up for tea…extra sweet.
Said they've cousins in Nineveh,
modern Mosul, on the Tigris.
That's nice.
Not in the least,
unless you like car bombs and dead kids.
Apologies to your tea-buddies.
Oh they're used to the likes of you.
What do you mean, the likes of me?
They had Jonah down there once,
all grim and prophesying doom.
A tad late, but guess he was right…
A shrill little man with bad breath…
Whale bile, see; it does that to you.
Funny, sounds just like the VP.
A few inhibitors and a hand-job
that might have stopped all the trouble.
So that's how you treat your patients…
No, most of them self-medicate.
So what happened to old Jonah?
Buried in a hill, with whale bone.

Home Sweet Home.

They sat on the bench, beneath a map:
The Drake, Chicago, Sunday at eight…
Alright, and how *is* your lovely wife?
She signed… I have nudunnu,
perfumes to pour upon your head.
Sent her back to daddy, then?
Mother was livid, her lotus curled shut.

She wouldn't have you near her, see,
defiled as you are by work,
but my future is with you.
Is that an assumption agreement,
Or a proposal?
Does it matter?
Yes, I do.

A tango to the withered gourd...

Trays for Days (Chuva)

April 2001

From a tower of glass
he sat long and watched
the river's chug,
its curdled tumble.
      São Paulo
Five-star glaze and steel
neoclassical creamstone
plywood shanties.
An April evening
stained with Tuesday
Brown and crusty,
Autumn pale.
      Nine pm
Over southern spit-roast,
at a house of illustrious repute,
nonpublic thoughts were shared
and futures read in spreads of M&As
and rolled securities,
while backscratching girls
milked them for college fees,
and Louis Vuitton bags.
Clasps and tongues loosened
in puffs of Cuban
and Scotch spittle.
We give ergo receive:
gods, traders, escorts.
Anyway
They play *choro* there
in Rio,
beneath the arches of Lapa,
but here the music never cries,
but rains.

Alex gazes out across the river,
A brown, capybara-and-concrete chute.
The sky here is a constant threat of rain,
of a traffic-stalling deluge, cloud to drain.
It's the Big Bad Wolf in a lighting ball
blowing down the house with a sudden squall.

Alex watches from the window, all-proof, air-tight.
His whiskey eyes overexpose the light,
drag it out like a Chinese ribbon dance,
— the tail-lights flap, the headlights prance.
But her reflection, framed in bathroom glow,
Congeals upon the bed, all lace and tone.
Her elastic adjusted, she lies down prone,
Blows away a strand of hair, sets aside her phone.

All waxed and silken, liner round the eyes,
designer nails, tattoos, muscular thighs,
A luxury item, rented like a tux,
She wraps him up in an automated flux.
But is that thing a river? Does it flow?
A graywater crush, so still and shallow...

[Morning after, Hotel bar]
Alex, drained and knowing,
but none the wiser,
thanks the secure server
and sips his coffee.
His laptop, a swamp of quads,
deafened by decimals,
and mountainscape graphs;
            just as in London or Berlin,
            Berlinda, Lindoningren,
            Shanghai and Dublin,
            Semi-new Delhi, Istan on
            Bull, Paris-Aberystwyth.

In the lobby, piped waves of bossa nova
and clocks on the walls for every time zone.
But it's fair day outside, full of local tone
and color, the land's offerings stacked on stalls,
fresh from the earth, the trees, the trellised walls.
A traveling circus where the seller bawls:
Três por dez
Pears, pineapples, siriguela
Três por dez
Jenipapo, cupuaçu…
Trays for days
Caju, cambuci, mandacaru

So Alex Iden Gray
ventures jungle through:
A Wallace in Tocantins
A Bates on the Solimões
A bandeirante, a missionary punk
A French landscaper, a Jesuit monk,
Bringing order to the Oca,
Pruning all those rowdy trees.
and Alex Iden studies all,
left and right:

Earth

      abundance
      bounty

Abounding

But this is a very vertical land,
top-down, with accusing, expectant
upward glances, mouths agape.
And Alex, alone in the crowded fair,
watches the rainclouds, like burgeoning thoughts,
come musing over rooftops, nimbly darkening
and reaching for words. The wind rushes,
the tarpaulin flaps, the old women quicken,
muttering skyward:

      Alex Iden Gray,
      shall we slay the bull,

hindleg to foreleg,
bound upon a spit
and rolled over fire?

And Alex answers with the black lips of mind

I see an aurochs
running on the plains,
drawing predators,
thirsty parasites.
Running with its kind.
The arrows sting.
It stands and bleeds.
The blood flows, its
breathing labors.
It shakes a warm mist,
shrouding its face,
and rolls a calm eye
which will never blink.
I can see its blood
smeared above your door

Skinning

Its ballsack nailed
to your threshold,
Its hide and horns
worn in a dance,

Flame

wild, around a red flame.
Its immolation
pays for this bounty,
worthy of a thousand gleaming bodies
smeared with ash.

Returning

The smell of burning flesh:

The budget solstice, duly observed, decrees
that the harvest gods shall not smile broadly this House,
but neither shall they scowl nor brawl.

And in April, they shall gather Tribute

The smell of rain:

Water

back to salt and mud and rock back from cirrus **ice** and cloud at six **thous**and meters above ground in the rare air where the light breaks falling falling **falling** to wash the blood and dirt from the land falling falling back to the minerals and acids the gutters the puddles and pools and potholes to roll off the blades of leaves trickling pinball through tree boughs to the undergrowth and topsoil frogbacks insect wings furry shoulders and feathers back to **river**heads and **moun**tain streams bogs and mangroves to rockpools and lakes **wells** and reservoirs to be drunk and sprayed piped and drained back to meltwater and washwater heat transfer to soothe and heal and bathe anoint baptize back from the **wisps** the haze breathed around the globe in swirls back to ice and snowflakes drifts and frost stormwater skimmate sewage and amniotic fluid back to refracted light divided into bows wrapped around gifted landscapes back to the reefs and **under**ground caves back to asphalt and tire grooves runoff with dead leaves dead papers bubble spit urea rolling seeping gus**hing** dripping sinking soaking percolating gnawing absorbing and eroding washing in and washing out carrying and depositing creating and destroying drowning and giving life entering and being entered surrounding and bei surrounded following the to**ngue** of the moon across rippling waves kneading and knowing the alleys and gul**lies** blowholes and crevices trenches a rambling murmuring string of **drops-**hazes-flakes falling and rolling freezing and boiling rising and waiting and ahhhh the unbearable **light**ness of peeing all the way back and still you **do** not listen, Alex, **TAXI TAXI do** not heed TAXI **TAXI** *TAXI TAXI* though you hear and even taste the **color** of my barely audible **s**pin and spill and sop and waft and **rise** from the **asp**halt into sky

Wind

Inner Truth

Joust and Tell

April 1999

Thames-side,
gamesmen play toss
against the walls
      of parliament,
flicking trilobites
      against the Clipsham.
They tourney and vie
      where elephants once roamed
          Embankment.
They joust with stratagems
and swing their tricks like maces.

A spread of wands, cups, and shields,
my three aces beat your queen
to bishop. They compensate
for my fallen tower and felled knight.

Alex goes to the deck
for a Fool of all four trades,
known all along the Silk Road.
Your joker shoelaced my rook,
burnt it to the ground with Roman candles.
Rock breaks scissors, paper wraps the rock...

But I'll blow the whizzer on all your cons.
call Immigration on all your pawns.

There'll be a right royal flush,
and that's checkmate in two.

Oh sourpuss, huffing buffalo.
No sore losers in hardball.

**

April 1999

An AWACS radar plane
slides like a stethacanthus shark
through the carboniferous murk
of London sky,
Heading off to Kosovo.

Alex descended into the whale
at Embankment. He changed cetacean
at Leicester Square,
and was spat onto the sands
at Covent Garden,
where a bar grew up around him,
giving shelter.

On a stool, there was a paper:
The Daily Mirror Mail of the Independent Standard Guardian Sun:
MACEDONIAN BORDER CLOSED

Borders—
       Beringia, a Laurasian kiss,
       the ark of a furry Noah.
       A yawn of ice to walk across.
       Eocene Eurasia, an archipelago in shallow seas.
       Australia
           – Gondwana
       South America
           – Gondwana
       Antarctica
           – Gondwana
       The Hrt f frc
           Sing the stolen vowels of frc
    e a o A i a

e a o A i a
       all Gondwana
Hindia
The crumpled Himalayas,
       – Gondwana
The Turgai Strait,
       its Cretaceous sharks,
A jigsaw world spread apart.

But that camp at Blace,
pure pestilence: bursting with Kosovars,
and Poles, at elbows with the Roma,
and the Tutsis, the Rwandans
and Cathars, Sierra-Leone boys
and the Mina off slave ships.
All those Tibetans and Aborigines,
Amerindians and Palestinians,
such an almighty mess, and more
still coming, from Kurdistan,
Afghanistan, Mongolia and Antioch,
from Troy and all the burning cities,
fleeing crosses, winged lions,
swastikas, golden eagles,
cardinal stars.

MACEDONIAN BORDER CLOSED
BELGRADE BURNS

War is the methadone of the people.
Guilty TV with night-vision cumshots,
as pounded buildings collapse
on the pillows of rumpled streets.

The Russians reach Eggersdorf,
a neanderthal gathers flowers for fresh graves.

KosovoColorado
Trench coats and flak jackets

London Spring, warm feathers on a cold bird,
a grey reflection settles undisturbed
on the broad pane of a bookstore window.
Alex checks his hair, slicks a quiff of shadow
where outspoken titles tumble and pile
or stand to attention in single file:
shells of memoir with their soft-bellied truths
and dirty knickers in confession booths.
This time next month another exposed spine
will carry a title on Columbine.
How fast it moves, never missing a beat,
from hardcover charge to soft-back retreat.
At war, not *in* war, the rubble is books,
shrinkwrapped on palettes and loaded on trucks.

But Alex is in wonderland,
so off with all their heads.

THE DAILY WHALE

FRIDAY APRIL 23, 1999

Belgrade Burns

A wolf climbed Kosmaj Mountain and saw, on the distant ocean, a tremendous sea monster spitting stinging flies from its mouth. The flies, or perhaps they were wasps, or hornets, flew in from the ocean and burned the towns with flames. Sources close to the wolf say she was dismayed by the thundering noise and feared dreadfully for her new -born cubs.

It seems a baleful spirit has fallen upon the land, and the humans roam in haggard, starving bands, driven along by hyenas in uniform. The wolf, who has long been a studi -ous observer of human behavior, is convinced those in camouflage jackets have turned to cannibalism. They have also taken to hoarding the bodies of their kills so they can find them and dig them back up in the winter.

"Very poor form from the humans here", says the wolf, who had thought people had more honor. "Year after year, their conduct deteriorates, and the spirit of the land grows weak."

cont. page 3

Elephants on Embankment

Strange news for Londoners this evening, as reports emerge of several large straight-tusked eleph -ants seen roaming along Embank -ment. Last seen on British shores over ten thousand years ago, the species has long been considered...

Theotaurotokos

July 1995

Alex Icarus the Gray
was something else.
A minor legend with failsafe wings.
Quite the whizz, the protege.
Just the man for that call from Belgrade,
From a lady with a plan:
>"Build me a labyrinth of hedgerows,
>but build me first a cash cow,
>a comely cow to excite the bull.
>I shall wait inside her, ágape."
As in a fresco of frolic and folly,
the Lady had him leap the bull,
with flips and pirouettes.
After all, that was their job,
as architects of mazes,
The keepers of complex hedgerows:
to leave the bull in a swoon.

She was an unusual woman, this Serb,
and the Bull's eye, ascertained,
roused robust investments,
copious deposits,
and the wrath of her defrauded lord.

Over on Vanderbilt,
they opened a bottle of Krstač
and toasted bounty and high yields.
Yes, futures smoldered all around,
But there was not a single floating feather.
No melted wings among the wreckage.

Many a minotaur is born from maculate conceptions.

Pasiphae, the Taurotokos,
rocking her beast in her lap,
receives quarterly annunciations
and progress reports from her men on the ground.

Glistening sunlight fills the church
                Lady Wideshine kneels to pray.
Above her hangs the Second Ark
                gleaming bright in silver plate,
and in those arms the Covenant,
                Word unspoken, still unheard,
Theotokos, splendrous in blue,
                knows the damage words can do.
So Lady Pious drops her gaze
                cowed beneath that piercing stare
as rolling somewhere on the floor,
                lidless, with an ancient musk,
Pandora's pithos empties out,
                spills its apples on the stone,
A gust of wind inebriates
                Serpentine its olive tone.

Protection zone
        Overrun
Request for air support
        Denied

Their villages torched and burned
                Bosniaks flee into the woods,
As Serb troops prowl the hills like wolves.
                Srebrenica, the 'safest' place,
has crowds encamped at compound gates.
                "Make sure they hear their screams,
and know just what is being done,
                see the mattress by the wall
and learn to cower, hold their tongues."

Soldiers march the men away
Round the zinc works to open graves,
scores of them, all freshly made.
The Dutchbat watch and stay inside.
Girls are singled out for rape.
The Dutchbat watch and stand aside.
Laughing soldiers do their worst,
the worst men do when stops are pulled;
Huffing and puffing with the wind
like scared monkeys in a storm.
Where Pietà weeps and waits.
A Serb, irate, a woman warns:
"Stop that baby's whingeing, bitch!"
Machine guns cackle on the hills.
"Shut that baby's goddamned mouth."
The men are gone, the women brace:
"Shut that baby's trap or else!"
and now she rocks a silenced child
soaked in drying crimson robes.
The Lady lights a candle wick,
watches as the flame unfolds,
The mother clad in silver robe,
knows the sculpture, set the mold.

Taurokatharpsia

October 23, 4004 BC

Calm sky
groaning herds
droplets of dew
on grass blades
weak sun,
watercolour,
early morning haze.
Tall grass
swatting tails
petulant hooves
on wet banks.
Fat tongues
morning thirst
animals in ranks.
Necks shake
warning horns
nostrils muster
a dull bray;
wet mist
a billowing
ordinary day.

On the sixth,
he woke with wounds:
a slit in the side;
defensive lacerations
on hands and forearms.
She stared back, unbegotten

blinked the sun into a ball
and all was well.

JONAH'S MAP OF THE WHALE

*

October 23, 1989 – bell ring

It ends as it starts, at a dollar and six a bushel.
The three sisters in a huff.
Relations frosty.
Tighten your corn belt,
for winter promises.

Trailer lady, first-born in the corn,
placenta buried at a scarecrow's feet,
she sucks smoke and blows out curses
at the ring of low pressure bills
and rumbling arrears groaning on the plains.
And that deadbeat, slowmo son of hers,
conceived out on Powder Horn
to a big guy with a small dick.
That tool just sits there fishin' bass,
skinny legs dangling off the pier,
counting the corns on his reflected feet.
Go walk like Jesus, boy, who can't swim none,
go walk out to them boats…
Or into Little Arizona desert
for forty scorpion days of snakebite and change.
Those backlit eyes, always shifting,
always batting and blinking.
A lumberjack with an ermine's head,
her furry manboy, like a fairground prize
won for shooting ducks off a rack,
pulled from a shelf from under nine months of dust.
At least the girl helps out
when she ain't pullin' double shifts and cowboys.

But that thing that's turning is no Ferris wheel.
No water wheel, no windmill.

Aleph, mem, shin, ftse, nasdaq, dow,
the currencies float on lotuses

*

October 23, 1989 – horn blow
Mechanical bull
hard buck and spin
He dusts himself off
with a silly grin
and bounds from the mat
to jeers and applause.
Rubs his ass with theatrical pause
and orders a pitcher of beer.

Well lookie here
Ain't you the last sheaf in the field.
I'm gonna take you home for the winter, doll.
Say, you know what corn ticker is?
Had this tattooed on my heart, see.
Ticker on the ticker, so to speak
        C84I@292\'5
Pretty ain't it?
What's it mean?
It means money honey...
Yeah, okay, I wrote that on there with a marker,
But we could get tattoos, you and me,
Alex and....*Carline.*
Carline and Alex up a tree,
H-U-M-P-I...Ouch, baby…

*

October 24, 1989 – card punch

She nets her tassel
and straightens her stalk
for a windy day, after a breezy night.
The rustle is loud at the conveyor belt:
"Carline bedded the Jolly Green Giant"
Oh shush now, let the girl speak…
"A jolly, windy, whispering thing it was too,
all tenderloins and brisket".
Did he lick your silk and part your husk,
dribble your blades with bull musk?
It wasn't like that…
Of course not, buckaroo.
How long'd he stay on for?
Did he make the buzzer?
A triumph of performance *and* design.
The giddy girls in whites and gumboots
hose down the aluminum, shrinkwrap the slabs,
bin the fat caps and muscle straps,
and off it goes for Adamic labelling
carved in Osirian parts.
Well, you gonna see him again?
Halloween ball at his firm next week,
I'm goin' as Wilma Flintstone…
Yabba dabba doo

*

Tauroctony,
Mithras in his smurfy hat
mounts the Bull, seized by the Elnath,
grabbed by the iron-age horn.
The knife finds the artery
And slices a gurgling mouth,
Whispering in bloody mysteries
Of wine and wheat.
The dog is friend, the snake is foe,
But both lap the Bull's blood,
both partake in the spilled life.
The scorpion, more ancient,
All inside-out, goes for the life unspilled,
the seed in the Bull's ballsack.

The sun watches from its chariot
The raven, from its perch.

The twins, with their torches, attend at the seacave
Where blood yields wheat, and wheat requires blood.

Nausea

July 1985

He took her to a movie at the multi-complex
one popcorn blowjob weekday evening.
She licked her lips and asked for water,
brushed her hair back from her round face.

He asked her, songlike, if he was the only one.
Ruby grinned and cooed oh-you're-jealous – which he was –
and kissed his cheek, with appreciation and warning:
Of course you are, she replied, with backscatter.

Later, astride an older man,
her voice cracked to oil,
and seeped to the surface:
   I want to bear your wife and be your child,
   made with each other, we were… made with each other….made…

   Everyone is an only one.

And the sun saw the dampened wind waves,
the dark patches;

Clac Clac Cloaca

I'll need the books back soon, Alex, she said.
There's more to life than math, you know!
Science can fly us away to the moon,
but the abyss travels with us, wherever we go.

Iron in the Soul, he'd managed half.
But *Nausea* had lived up to its name.
As for *Being and Nothingness*, he was stuck somewhere
on section II of the Introduction.

Read and be freed, Alex.
Read and be freed, she said:
Existence before essence!

When the news slicked of the senior partner
in Ruby's affections, his mercury rose;
a ring of high pressure parked above his halo,
skewing the Westerlies. His mind warmed,
and sensitive structures, bleaching and brittle,
spilled their zoox, destroying the habitats
of colorful notions. The rock grew drab and bare,
leaving only crabs to sift amongst the silt.

Ruby Controllop, snared in a net,
resented the interruption:

*We are not what we are
and are what we are not.*

It was only logical, of course:
Computers were becoming personal;
people, computational.

One day, Alex, she said, taking his hands in hers.
When you're a married man, and a daddy,
with your two-point-five and a mutt,
and your badass job and big-ole house
in a fenceless garden in a walled-in suburb,
and you stare into that Sunday morning mirror
as the deLorean of memory comes screeching up outside,
the flames still crackling in its tire tracks,
It'll be me you come back to, honey.
To me, and my *générosité*.

Later that year, they found the RMS *Titanic*,

and the space shuttle *Atlantis* made its maiden voyage.
So did Nintendo and Windows 1.0.

World population was just shy of five billion.
And Alex was twenty-one.

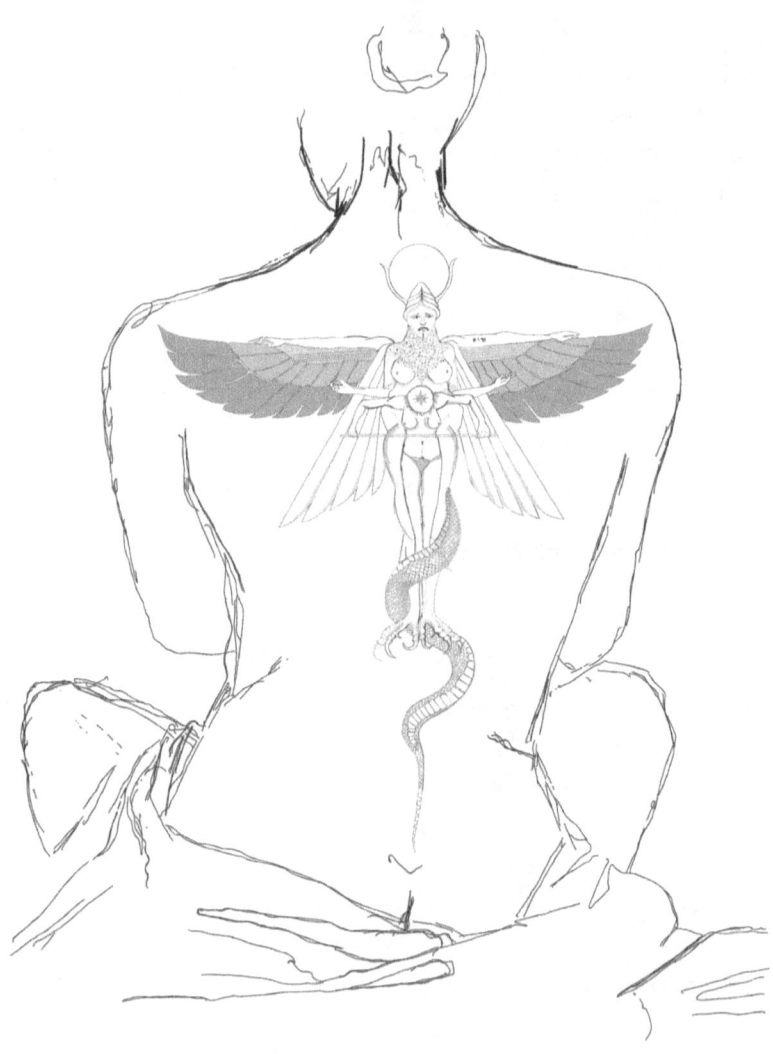

Ruby's Being and Nothingness

(The) _____ only come(s) into the world
through beings who are their own _____;
for whom (their own) _____ is/are an issue.

- ✓ Being
- ✓ Nothingness
- ✓ Time
- ✓ Space
- ✓ Lack
- ✓ Possibility
- ✓ Good
- ✓ Evil
- ✓ Past
- ✓ Present
- ✓ Future
- ✓ Other(s)
- ✓ Multiplicity
- ✓ Ontology
- ✓ Morality
- ✓ Politics
- ✓ Ethics
- ✓ Aesthetics
- ✓ Death
- ✓ Thought
- ✓ Feeling
- ✓ Intuition
- ✓ Sensation
- ✓ Sex

- ✓ Self
- ✓ Shadow
- ✓ Desire
- ✓ Imagination
- ✓ Words

Three-pirate Sing-along

April 26, 2018

Three figures sit on a gentle dune.
Yo ho ho and a bottle of rum.

and sing the blues to a merry tune.
Yo ho ho and a bottle of rum.

Old Alex Idle Graybeard, ouarrrr!
The scurvymost knave these parts by far,
worst blackguard as ever wore a scar,
hither he shuffles along the strand
swiggin' applejuice from Edenland
and mumbling curses to beat the band.
Yo ho ho and a bottle of rum.

Rest yer weary bones and square us four.
We saw as your body washed ashore.
Yo ho ho and a bottle of rum.

You went a-swimmin' to drown yer sin
but all you lost was yer lower pin,
a toothpick in a bullshark's grin.
Billowy red the water roiled,
the ocean frothin', the waves all coiled,
and you was practically uncted and oiled
Yo ho ho and a bottle of rum.

But ye 'scaped the snapper's jaws o' death,
Ye gagged and gobbed and gasped for breath.
Yo ho ho and a flagon of rum.

He turned upon them a squinting eye,
spied them thricetimes, and none too shy,

Half-expecting it was all a lie:
'If ye be false, the lord strike ye dead'.
'He already did, for truth', he said,
the one with the crown atop his head.
Yo ho ho and a

'I'll second that', said the Copper-age bum,
as the third one sat and sucked his thumb.
Yo ho ho and a bottle of rum.

Yo ho.

Ho.

So Alex, you brought the storm upon them
and they threw you from the boat.

They threw you from the boat,
they made you walk the plank.

Remember, Alex; remember and recall.

And from the depths
where sense is an empty shell,
he drew his deepest memories from Jones' locker:

"There was a lobster in the toilet
just before I flushed.
A lobster, livid red, old and plated.
I remember it clear as day,
chitin on porcelain, legs a-scuttle
Tap…tappetty-tap…tap…tap.

"I was told, and can contend,
that the dead assume the shape of a cross.
Shot cowboys knocked from rooftops roll into a cross.

Shouldn't graves be dug in the shape of a cross?

"I've been hiding for hours and hours on end.
I thought they'd have missed me by now,
sent out search parties to find me.
I've been curled on top of this wardrobe
for what feels like an afternoon.
The room looks different from up here.
with a ghost's-eye view of my bed.

"When I built a robot in my uncle's yard,
out of junk and scrap, saw-offs, leftovers,
it had all the parts, only the life was missing.
I found some wires and circuit board in the shed,
and fixed him a heart, but the heart wouldn't beat.
So I put it in its head, but the head wouldn't think.
Shouldn't the whole be the sum of its parts?

"On the rim of sleep, the bed fills with ocean,
I can't stretch my legs, it's too cold and deep.
The soles of my feet expect the rub
of sandpaper skin, my calves
the inquisitive tug of maw, my waist
the embrace of projectable jaws.

A dead bird. What's its secret?
A dead fish… just circuit board with fins.
A busted rat… Turkish delight spread for crows.

Mother was stern.
Death is the absence of life, my boy.
Like darkness is the absence of light.

And dreams are lanterns.

Make no mistake:
Hearts are not heartbeats.
A broken heart is a heart that grew bones.
Spine in a heart, ribs round the chambers,
talons clutching each lung.
Those are the hearts that break.

"Only the life was missing"
Everything else was there.

"I flushed down the lobster,
I curled up my legs to sleep,
I knocked the tin-man over
and buried his bits in the reeds."

Yo ho ho, and a six-ounce by the rail
tracks.
A swish of ember and regret.

Alex stumbles lame
          from the glare.
His eyes, twin holes in a painting,
watching from the wall
as great whales shrink to pinpricks
          in the blue.

A return, now, to the beachfront house,
to the market news in real time…
Real time? We know the true meaning
of neither word.

Alex would rather watch it all burn.
But there is always somewhere
we'd rather see destroyed than saved.

"Now where can I find some life?"

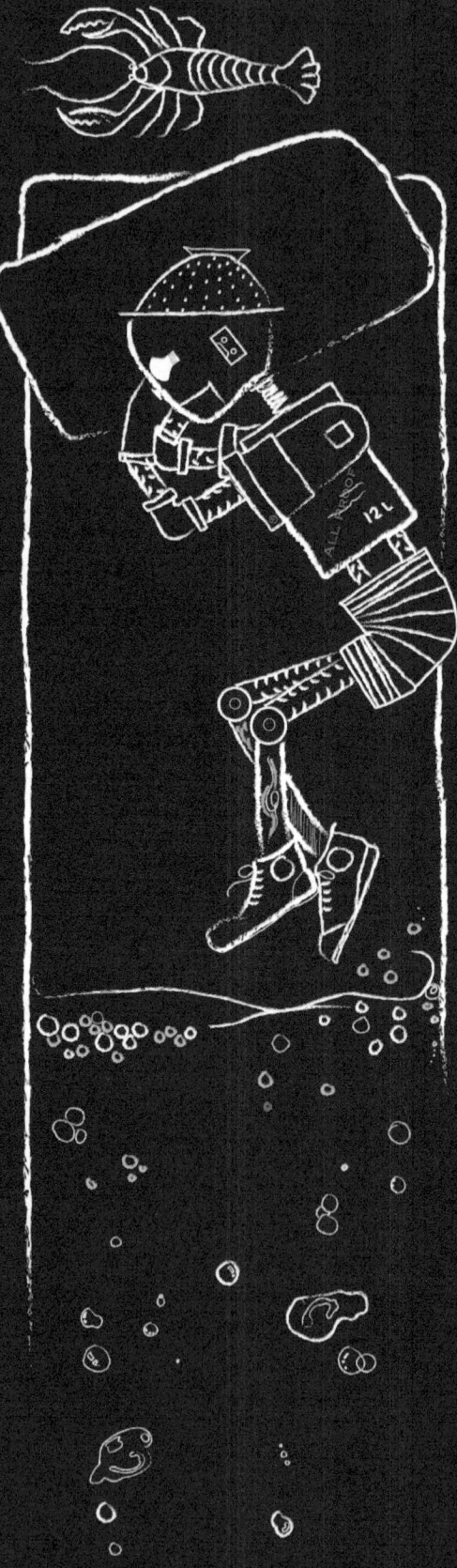

Bullish on this.
In your own private Nineveh.
Drive your arrogant king from the gates
in sackcloth.
Make his shadow grow like a gourd on the hot sand
to give him shelter.
Make him kneel and repent,
until the Temple fills again with wind.

The three, their vigil ending, salute the departing shape.
      a ridge of fin.
      a spread of tail.
Disturbed water
      quickly resettles.
And Alex is hurled toward his own absence.
Thrown, again. Thrown back.
Eyes wide, language speaking.

Drive your arrogant king from his throne.

He opens and closes a hand.
Blinks the hospital daylight.
Tastes the thirst in his mouth.

Throw the tall gates open to the wind.

He tries to move a leg that isn't there,
And remembers the smash, the crunch, the tear.

The shark in the darkened water.

And he waits for the pain to wake.

Westward they roll....

Acknowledgments

A special thank you to Dianne Pearce and David Yurkovich, whose mission means a tremendous amount to a lot of people.

Thanks to my fellow Old Scratch Press members: Alan Bern, Ellis Elliott, R. David Fulcher, Gabby Gilliam, Morgan Golladay, Nadja Maril, Robert Fleming, Dianne Pearce, Virginia Watts.

About the Author

ANTHONY DOYLE is an Irish writer and translator.

He is the author of the speculative sci-fi novel *Hibernaculum* (Out Of This World Press, 2023), an NGIBA Finalist, and two children's books, *O Lago Secou* (Companhia das Letrinhas, 2013) and *O Livro das Sereias Surpreendentes* (Grua, 2025), which represents his first outing as an illustrator.

Anthony lives in São Paulo (Brazil) with his wife, daughter, cat, three dogs, guinea pig and assorted fish.

He is one of the founding members of the short-form collective Old Scratch Press. This is his first volume of poetry.

Welcome to a future where human hibernation is a way of life.

"THOUGHT-PROVOKING SF DELIVERED IN AN INTRIGUINGLY PANORAMIC FORM."
KIRKUS

ANTHONY DOYLE
HIBERNACULUM
A NOVEL

where the new you begins

Anthony Doyle's "Hibernaculum"

A Dystopian in which time is money, time is trouble, and time is risk.

Available in hardcover, paperback, eBook, and audiobook formats
at Amazon and other online booksellers, and select bookstores.

Copyright ©2023 Anthony Doyle. All rights reserved. Published by Devil's Party Press, an imprint of Current Words Publishing, LLC.

www.ingramcontent.com/pod-product-compliance
Lightning Source LLC
Chambersburg PA
CBHW021652120626
46545CB00002B/817